5 STEPS TO RETIREMENT PLANNING

Actions You Can Take to Achieve Your Retirement Goals

Louis Green, CFA®, CFP®, CPWA®

TABLE OF CONTENTS

INTRODUCTION

WHY RETIREMENT PLANNING MATTERS AND THE *5-STEP APPROACH*

Why Retirement Planning Matters

Retirement planning often feels like standing at the edge of an uncharted ocean. The idea of navigating financial security, investment choices, and lifestyle changes can be daunting. Whether you are already retired or approaching retirement, it is easy to feel overwhelmed by the sheer magnitude of what is needed for retirement.

You probably have one or more of the following questions: How much will I need to retire comfortably? Will I ever run out of money? Do I have enough money saved for emergencies? How should I manage my money? Should I use a wealth advisor? What will the tax bite be on my income in retirement? Do I need an estate plan?

These questions can be paralyzing. Defined contribution plans, which are employer-sponsored retirement plans that task employees with choosing their own investments, continue to be the dominant choice for employers.[1] The message is clear: we are responsible for our own retirement.

Number of Pension Plans by type of plan, 1975-2022[1]

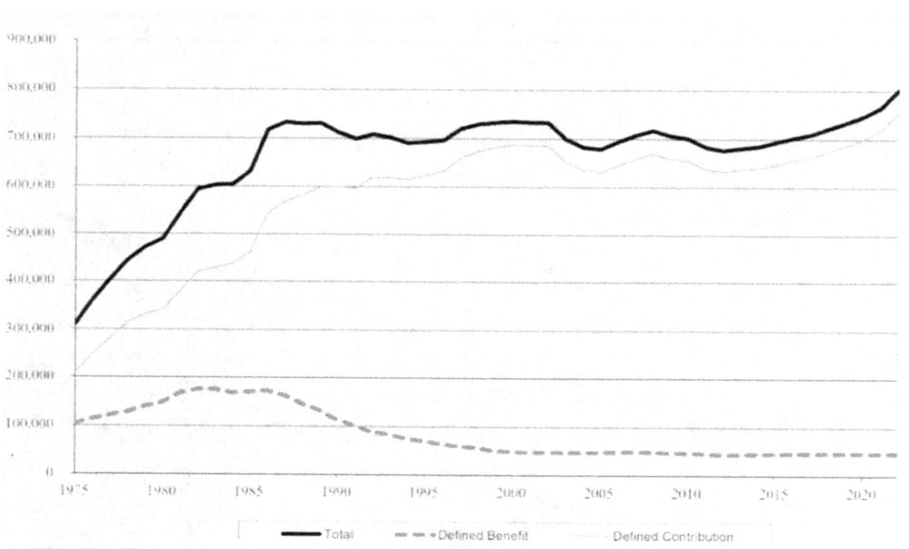

Retirement planning is not only about setting money aside; it is about ensuring that every aspect of your future is examined in detail so that you can enjoy retirement without worry.

While retirement planning might seem intimidating, having the right approach can make things easier for you. If you break down the process into manageable steps, you can transform retirement planning into a series of achievable goals.

The 5-Step Approach

This eBook is designed to guide you through five essential steps: Financial Planning, Investment Planning, Tax Planning, Estate Planning, and Lifestyle Management. Each step is a compass to steer you through the fog of uncertainty and toward a clear, confident retirement.

First, we will discuss financial planning. Financial planning will be the blueprint of your retirement plan. Next, we will discuss investment planning. Your investments are one of the primary vehicles you will use to pursue your retirement and financial goals. We will then move on to tax planning. Tax planning should be a primary consideration in all your decisions because a few smart moves have the potential to reduce your tax bill. We will also discuss estate planning. Estate planning will help you distribute your assets according to your wishes. Finally, we will discuss lifestyle management.

According to a study by the United Nations, our average life expectancies will only continue to rise.[2] You should be deliberate about your activities and lifestyle in retirement because the odds are you will have a long life to live post-retirement. So, let's embark on this journey together. With each step, you will gain clarity and control, turning what once felt overwhelming into a navigable path towards a fulfilling retirement.

United States Life Expectancy [2]

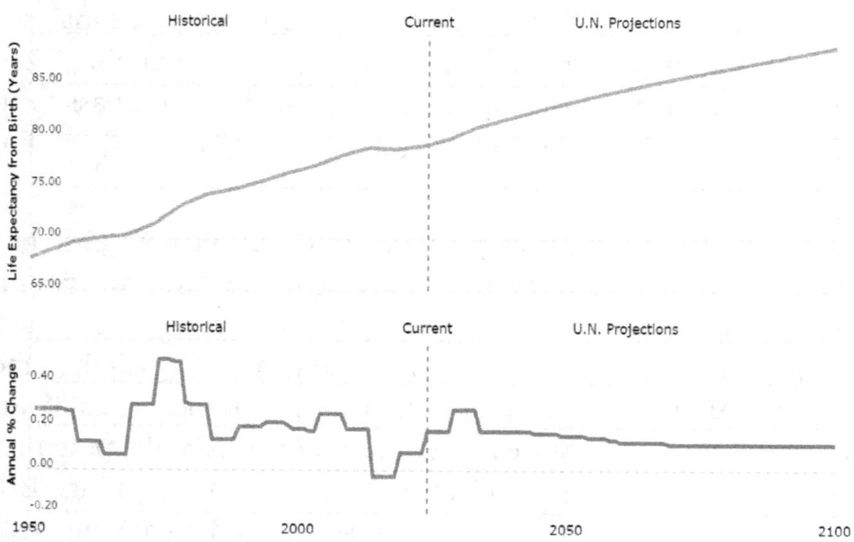

1 https://www.dol.gov/sites/dolgov/files/ebsa/pdf_files/private-pension-plan-bulletin-historical-tables-and-graphs.pdf

2 https://www.macrotrends.net/global-metrics/countries/CZE/uNITED-STATES/life-expectancy

STEP 1

FINANCIAL PLANNING: CREATING THE BLUEPRINT FOR YOUR RETIREMENT

Setting Retirement Goals

Financial planning is the foundation of a successful retirement. Creating and sticking to a financial plan is one of the best ways to start planning for your future. However, how do you know where to start? Start by setting your retirement goals. How much income will you need in retirement? What do you want to accomplish in retirement? Where do you want to live? What activities do you want to participate in? Are you looking to make a major purchase? If so, when and how much will it cost? How often do you want to travel? Do you feel travel is a necessity or something that is nice to do?

How about your hobbies? Whether you like to cook, dance, golf, or collect vintage wine, make sure to include a line in your budget for your hobbies.

Creating a Budget

Before you create a budget, start by creating a balance sheet and cash flow statement to capture your assets, liabilities, income, and expenses. These numbers will help you determine your current spending and net worth.

Next, create a budget that reflects your ideal spending. Some of your expenses (food, mortgage, medical etc.) are essential and probably can't be reduced. However, you might have some room to reduce discretionary expenses. Check your mortgage rate or the interest rates on any other loans you have to explore refinancing opportunities. Use a spreadsheet to track your actual spending versus your budget. Are you spending what you expected to spend? If not, why? Your next step is to project those expenses through retirement using a reasonable inflation rate. See the historical inflation rate below.

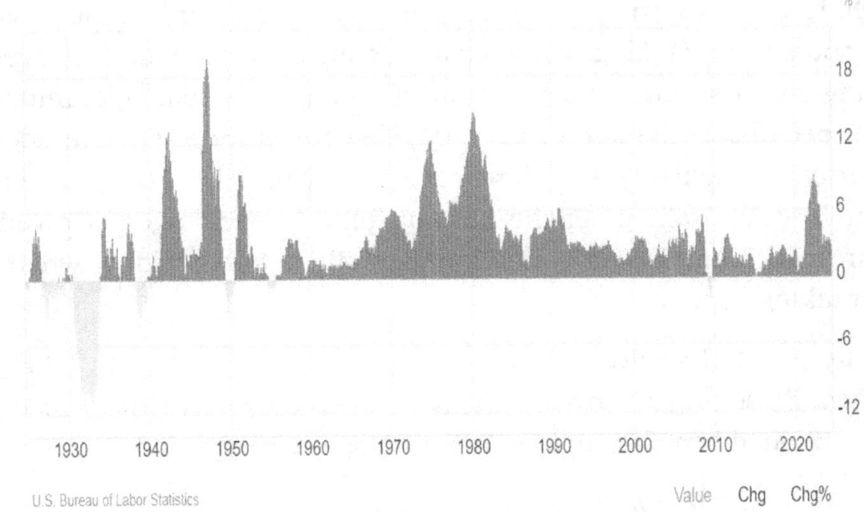

Create a Savings Plan

Whether you are just starting your retirement journey or newly retired, create a savings plan to pay yourself first. If you are just starting your retirement journey, use part of those savings to create an investment portfolio. Even the smallest portfolio can grow significantly over time with consistent contributions. Getting started now will allow you to reap the benefits of compounded interest over time.

Future Sources of Cash Flow

Consider your future sources of cash flow. Will you receive a pension? When will you start to take retirement account distributions? Project the future value of your assets using a conservative growth rate. Do not overestimate how large your portfolio will grow based off recent returns, and make sure to use average numbers. You will need these numbers to estimate future sources of cash flow.

Social Security

Include social security as a current or future source of income. If you are not currently taking social security, consider the tradeoffs between taking social security when you are first eligible versus maximizing your benefits at the age of seventy. You could increase your social security payments by an estimated 32% if you delay taking benefits until 70 versus taking benefits at your full retirement age.[4,5] Consider your financial and health situation carefully before deciding when to start taking benefits.

Set up a social security account at https://secure.login.gov/ to get started. By setting up an account, you can verify your earnings record, see estimated benefits, and apply for social security.

Monthly Benefit Based on Claiming Age [5]

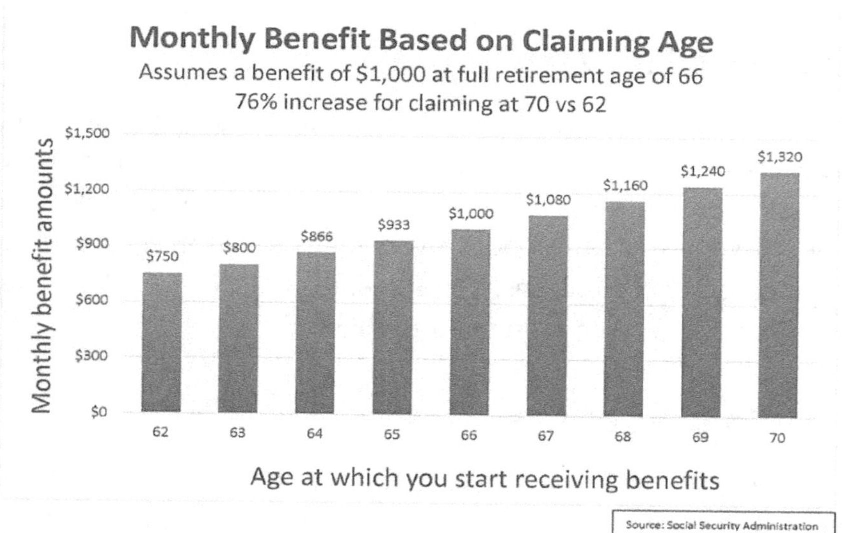

Sequence Risk

Having a plan to pay for your expenses in retirement is important because the amount you pull from your portfolio and the timing of those withdrawals are vulnerable to sequence risk, which is the risk of negative market returns right before or soon after you retire. Sequence risk is especially dangerous during the earlier years of your retirement if you are using a diminished portfolio to fund your living expenses. You should expect market volatility and structure your portfolio accordingly.

This is why you should pay special attention to your asset allocation, expenses, and emergency fund. In the next section, we will discuss how to create a goals-based portfolio to address sequence risk.

Withdrawal Rates

The amount you will need to pull from your portfolio will be one of the factors that determines how long your portfolio might last through retirement.

For example, the chart below represents two sample portfolios. Both portfolios started at $1,000,000 in July of 2004. Sample portfolio #1 (purple data line) had a 4% annual withdrawal rate over the following 20 years. Sample portfolio #2 (orange data line) had a 5% annual withdrawal rate over the same time period. As illustrated, the 4% portfolio ended with a value of $1.571 million, compared to $991,370.5 for the 5% portfolio – demonstrating a significant difference.

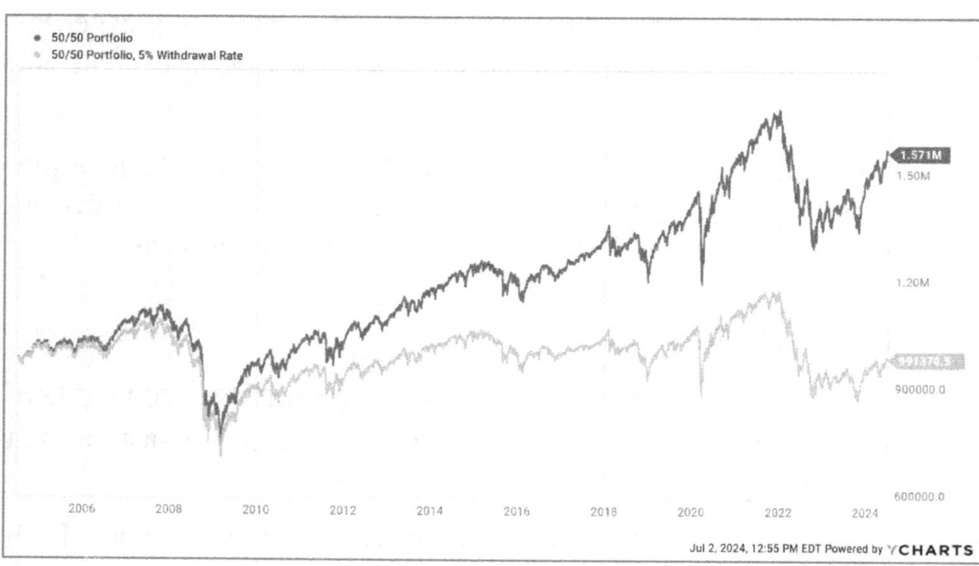

Hypothetical scenarios are for informational purposes only and do not represent an actual investor situation or actual outcome. All investments involve risk, including loss of principal. Past performance is not indicative of future results.

Managing Debt

Carrying debt into retirement can become a significant problem for you. If you have a large debt balance with a high interest rate on that debt, making only minimum payments can negatively affect your credit score and make it harder to get out of debt.[7] The payments needed to manage that debt in the future will use up vital resources.

Below are two hypothetical examples which illustrate the principal balance and interest payments made on a $15,000 credit card balance over time. Example 1 illustrates a $300 a month payment. Example 2 illustrates a $600 a month payment. As illustrated below in example 2, paying $600 a month significantly reduces the total interest paid and eliminates the debt in a little under 3 years versus almost 9 years for the $300 a month strategy.[8]

Example 1: Pay $300 a month on a $15,000 credit card balance with a 20% interest rate[8]

It will take **9 years and 1 month** to payoff the balance. The total interest is **$17,519.69**.

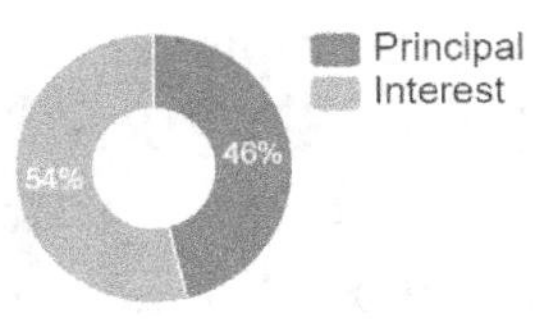

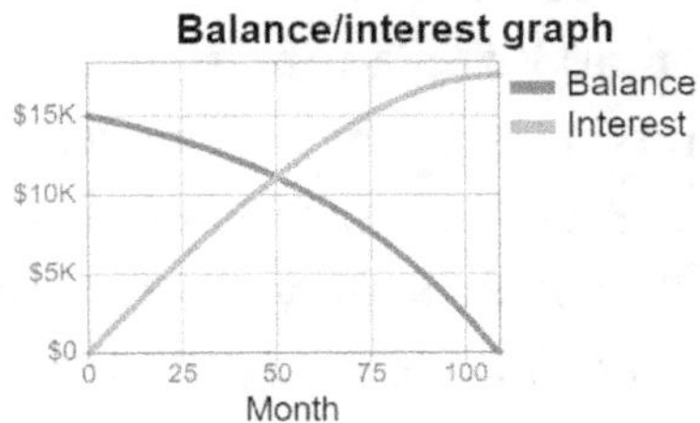

Example 2: Pay $600 a month on a $15,000 credit card balance with a 20% interest rate[8]

It will take **2 years and 9 months** to payoff the balance. The total interest is **$4,565.13**.

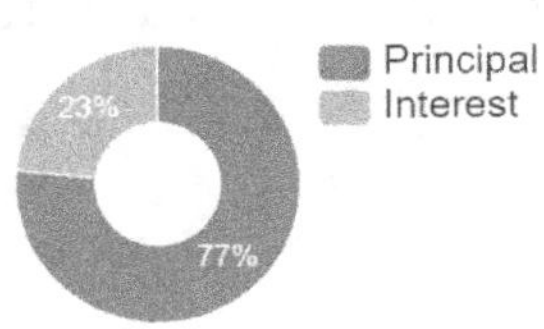

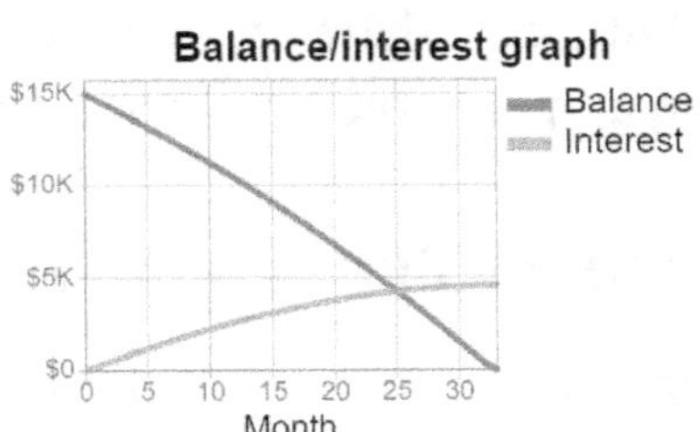

Source: Calculator.net

Create a plan to prioritize paying off high-interest debt first or build momentum by paying off smaller balances first. Include extra debt payments in your budget and identify savings or additional income (from a raise or bonus, for example) that you can use to reduce your debt.

Retirement Accounts

Funding a self-managed retirement plan or contributing to an employer-sponsored plan is one possible way to build long-term wealth. There are many options that are available for you. If you are eligible[9], you can fund a Traditional IRA or Roth IRA. Consider a 401(k) or 403(b) plan if either is available from your employer. If you are a business owner, consider a Solo 401(k) or SEP IRA. The requirements, funding levels, and benefits vary for each of these plans,[10,11] however they are all great ways to build a retirement plan and receive tax benefits. The tax benefits may include deductible contributions (Traditional IRA and/or 401(k) if eligible), tax free growth, and/or tax-free withdrawals (Roth IRA and/or Roth 401(k)).[9,10,11]

Funding a retirement plan and making annual contributions should be your priority. The sooner you start to fund one of these plans, the better off you may be in the long run. If your children are just entering the workforce, do them a favor and stress the importance of contributing to their retirement plan. Regular contributions to their retirement plan could be beneficial for them.

Emergency Funds and Liquidity

Retirement can bring unexpected expenses, and having a buffer can provide peace of mind. A good rule of thumb is to have 3-6 months' worth of expenses saved in an easily accessible account. Your emergency funds can cover anything from medical emergencies to home repairs. Your emergency fund should consist of liquid investments that can be sold quickly without significant fees or exposure to stock market declines.

Insurance

Insurance should play an important role in your financial plan. Life insurance, disability insurance, health insurance and property insurance should be core essentials of your plan. Consider umbrella insurance if you have a high risk of getting sued. If you are employed, you may be able to obtain disability and term insurance through your employer. Review all of your insurance policies annually to determine if you have adequate coverage.

Goals-Based Portfolio

Consider a goals-based portfolio that holds assets for a combination of your short-, medium-, and long-term goals. Any assets you need over the short term should be invested in lower risk assets such as a money market fund or short-term, high-quality bonds. Assets used to fund your intermediate goals can be invested more aggressively in a combination of intermediate bonds and equities. Finally, consider assets, such as alternative investments to fund long term goals, if you meet the investor qualifications and they are within your risk tolerance.

Challenges Unique to Professionals

Consider challenges that are unique to your profession. For example, if you are a medical professional, your student loans may have prevented you from funding an investment account. If debt is still a concern, create a plan to reduce your debt while also funding an investment portfolio. If you have a busy schedule, consider collaborating with an advisor who understands the unique challenges of your career and can accommodate meeting at a time convenient for you. Use virtual meetings to meet with your advisors if your time is limited.

If you own a medical practice, consider implementing extra insurance and asset protection strategies to protect yourself against lawsuits.

Restricted Stock and Stock Options

If you receive restricted stock or stock options, calculate how your holdings in employer stock (as a percentage) compare to your overall net worth. If you had to start from scratch, would you keep this allocation or would you diversify your investments?

Be mindful of the tax you must pay from the vesting of restricted stock awards. If you decide to sell some of your recently vested stock at a profit, you will be responsible for paying an additional tax on the proceeds from that sale. Look at all of your positions to determine the optimal position to sell. Look for positions that can be sold at an advantageous rate (long-term versus short-term capital gains rate), or even at a loss.

Business Owners

If you are a business owner, be mindful of the unique challenges and opportunities available to you. Consider pre-sale planning so that you are prepared when your company is sold. Consider a buy-sell agreement,[12] which will allow you and your partners to set a valuation for the business and create a process to sell portions of the business to other partners or back to the business itself. Buy-sell agreements are activated when a triggering event occurs, such as the death or disability of one of the owners.

Increase the attractiveness of your business by keeping all your documents in order, creating systems and processes, documenting the strengths, weaknesses, opportunities, and threats of the business, and ensuring that operations can run efficiently without you.

Fraud Protection and Digital Assets

Two other areas to consider are fraud prevention and digital assets. You should be on the lookout for frauds that can occur through the phone, email, or over the internet. Potential scammers have become increasingly sophisticated with their techniques. Do not share any information with anyone you do not recognize and watch out for anything that seems too good to be true.

Consider leaving instructions in your will or trust to address your digital assets. Take inventory of all your digital assets and leave usernames and passwords for your executor or trustee. Provide clear instructions around what you wish your loved ones to do with all your digital assets.

3 https://tradingeconomics.com/united-states/inflation-cpi

4 https://www.ssa.gov/benefits/retirement/planner/1943-delay.html

5 https://www.newyorklife.com/articles/make-the-most-of-social-security-benefits

6 YCharts. *50/50 Portfolio: 50% S&P 500 Total Return, 50% Bloomberg U.S. Aggregate Bond Index Total Return.* [July 2nd, 2024]

7 https://www.experian.com/blogs/ask-experian/what-happens-if-you-only-pay-the-minimum-amount-due/

8 https://www.calculator.net/credit-card-calculator.html?balance=15%2C000&rate=20&payoffoption=1&fixedpaymentamount=600&year=2&month=0&x=Calculate

9 https://www.irs.gov/retirement-plans/traditional-and-roth-iras

10 https://nb.fidelity.com/public/nb/default/resourceslibrary/articles/irslimits

11 https://www.investopedia.com/articles/financial-advisors/012716/solo-401k-vs-sep-which-best-biz-owners.asp

12 https://www.investopedia.com/terms/b/buy-and-sell-agreement.asp

STEP 2

INVESTMENT PLANNING:
BALANCING RISK AND RETURN

Investment Planning

Investment planning is one of the most important tools you can use to pursue your retirement goals. Investment planning begins with your asset allocation, which plays a big role in both the risk you take and the returns you may receive. Asset allocation is defined as the mix of assets you own, such as stocks (equities), bonds (fixed income), alternative investments, and cash.

Understanding Your Investment Options

Stocks and Bonds

One of the main building blocks of any portfolio is an investment in a company, municipality, or government entity. If you buy a company's stock, you become a partial owner. If you buy a bond, you are lending money to the company or entity in exchange for anticipated interest payments and the return of your money at a predetermined time.

There are many factors that may determine the value of your investments including, but not limited to, interest rates, inflation and company earnings reports. Market participants value companies with different metrics, such as the price-to-earnings ratio, which is defined as the current price of the stock divided by the past or future twelve months of earnings.

Mutual Funds and Exchange-Traded Funds

Rather than purchase shares of a company, you can purchase a mutual fund or an exchange-traded fund. Mutual funds and exchange-traded funds are similar in that they are baskets of stocks, bonds, or other assets professionally managed by a portfolio manager. You can also purchase an index fund, which aims to replicate an index such as the S&P 500 or Dow Jones Industrial Average. An index is a list of stocks that measures the performance of part of the stock market.

Exchange-traded funds offer intraday liquidity and are generally more tax efficient than mutual funds, which must redeem your shares directly back from you. These redemptions can create capital gains that are distributed to the mutual fund shareholders.

Separately Managed Accounts

Another option to consider is a separately managed account (SMA). An SMA is a professionally managed portfolio of individual bonds or stocks. Unlike mutual funds or exchange-traded funds, where you don't own the underlying shares, with an SMA, you own the individual shares. This ownership enables the SMA manager to harvest tax losses on your behalf, which could potentially lower your tax bill.

Direct Indexing

A direct indexing strategy is an SMA which seeks to replicate a stock index, such as the S&P 500, by purchasing some or all the companies within the index. Along with the tax benefits of harvesting losses, direct indexing gives investors the ability to tilt their portfolio away from the index and toward their preferences.

Investment Minimums

The investment minimums for SMAs and direct indexing tend to be higher than for exchange-traded funds or mutual funds.

Alternative Investments & Structured Notes

There are other strategies available for you to consider, provided you meet the minimum suitability criteria. Many of these strategies are highly illiquid and/or hold more risk, so they tend to require a minimum net worth, among other factors, to be deemed suitable for you.[13]

These strategies include structured notes, hedge funds, private equity, private credit, real estate, and commodities.

Structured Notes

A structured note is a pre-packaged investment that includes assets linked to a bond plus one or more derivatives, such as call and/or put options. A call option is a right to *purchase* a stock or index at a specific price. A put option is a right to *sell* a stock or index at a specific price. The derivatives are tied to an index or basket of securities and are designed to facilitate highly customized risk-return objectives.

Bonds typically aim to pay a combination of interest income and principal. A structured note replaces some of those payments with derivatives to provide a customized payoff based on the performance of an underlying index.

There are two primary types of structured notes - growth and yield notes.[14] Growth notes provide exposure to the returns of an index, which may or may not be capped at a certain level, along with partial or complete downside protection.

A yield note targets an income stream that is typically higher than you might receive in traditional bonds, along with some downside protection. They typically do not offer any upside appreciation above the yield you may receive.

Most of these notes are issued by a bank and there are exchange-traded funds that offer similar strategies.

You should strongly consider the drawbacks[15] before you purchase a structured note. Some of the drawbacks include liquidity, expenses, counterparty risk, index risk, and tax risk. While some structured notes provide partial or complete protection, please make sure you understand the terms of the note you purchase – all investments include risks. For example, if you sell a principal protected note prior to maturity, you could suffer a loss if the reference index has dropped in value.

Hedge Funds

Hedge Funds are financial partnerships that employ various strategies for their investors. Unlike most mutual fund managers, hedge fund managers typically have access to invest in a wide variety of assets and strategies. Hedge funds typically charge higher fees, offer limited liquidity, and the managers typically take a percentage of their profits (commonly referred to as performance-based fees). Hedge fund strategies include global macro, long short, relative value, and activist. You should be aware of the hedge fund strategy, fees, track record, and personnel before making an investment.

Private Equity Funds

Private equity funds are defined as a pool of money that a private equity firm uses to invest in private companies or special situations. Private equity funds are typically structured as a limited partnership, with the private equity firm acting as the general partner (GP) and the investors as limited partners. The GP's role includes evaluating potential investments and using the fund's capital to try to generate returns for the investors. These returns can come from a variety of strategies, such as improving operations or streamlining the capital structure. Private equity strategies include, but are not limited to, venture capital and leveraged buyout. Private equity funds are very illiquid and are typically considered for more long-term strategies. It's important to review the exit terms of private equity funds to fully understand terms and conditions associated with liquidity.

Private Credit

A private credit fund manager seeks to potentially earn a higher yield than might be available in the public credit markets by investing in non-publicly traded bonds. These higher yields come with extra risk, and it is the private credit manager's job to manage that risk. Some private credit strategies are less liquid than traditional investments.

Real Assets

Real assets include real estate, infrastructure, natural resources, and commodities, such as gold and silver. Real assets can be a good way to diversify a portfolio because their returns may provide a buffer from stock market returns in down years, depending on what the real asset is. Some of the asset classes, such as real estate funds, may also offer some protection against inflation as they pass along higher prices to consumers.

Risk Tolerance and Time Horizon

When structuring your investment portfolio, be mindful of your risk tolerance and time horizon. We define risk tolerance as your willingness and ability to accept risk. Some investors may have substantial wealth yet are *willing* to take on only minimal risk due to personal comfort levels. Other investors have a low *ability* to take on risk because they rely on their portfolio for immediate income needs.

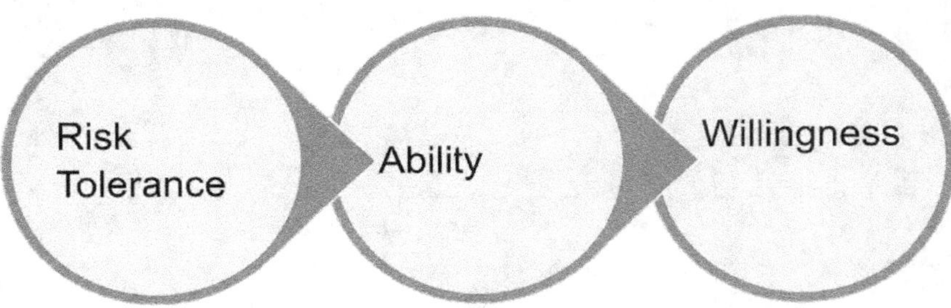

The following graph is an example of historical risk and returns for select portfolios.

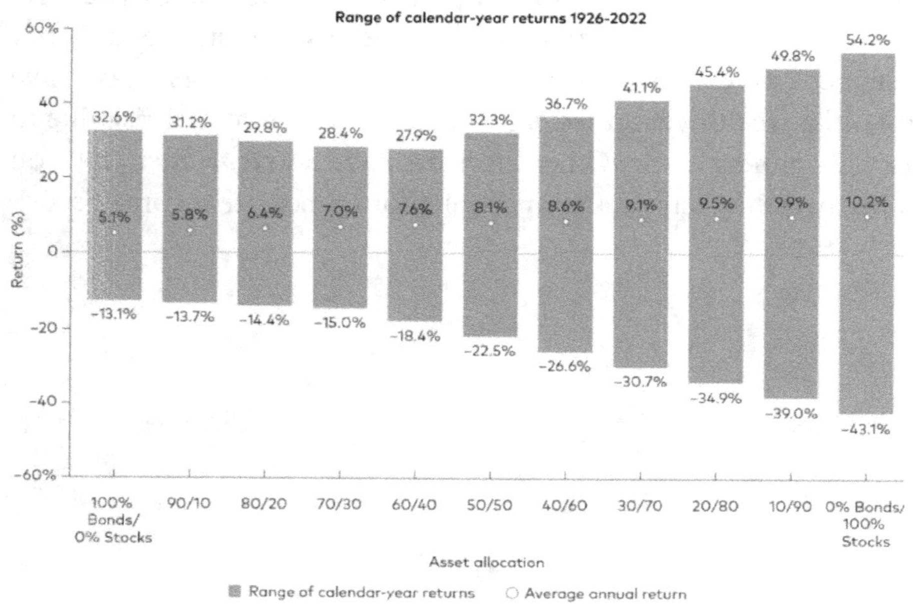

Source: Vanguard. Notes: Data for U.S. stocks is from Standard & Poor's 90 from 1926–1957, S&P 500 Index from 1957–1974, Wilshire 5000 Index from 1975–2005, MSCI US Broad Market Index from 2005–2013, and CRSP US Total Market Index from 2013–2022. Data for U.S. bonds is from Standard & Poor's High Grade Corporate Index from 1926–1968, Citigroup High Grade Index from 1969–1972, Lehman Brothers U.S. Long Credit AA Index from 1973–1975, Bloomberg US Aggregate Bond Index from 1976 –2009, and Bloomberg US Aggregate Float Adjusted Bond Index thereafter.

Past performance is no guarantee of future returns. The performance of an index is not an exact representation of any particular investment, as you cannot invest directly in an index.

Could you stay invested during turbulent times? Is your portfolio overly conservative? While it might be nice to have a safe portfolio when the markets are volatile, the projected returns of that portfolio might not help you meet your financial goals.

Building a Diversified Portfolio

Consider building a diversified portfolio to reduce risk and help balance returns. Be aware of how much of your portfolio is invested in a single asset class, strategy, or company. Consider how each asset class you own contributes to your portfolio. While over-allocating to an asset that has recently outperformed could provide short-term gains, you should consider what may happen if that asset suddenly starts to drop in value.

The following example from Y Charts illustrates the projected annual returns and risk for various portfolios.

Efficient Frontier: Your Current Portfolio vs. Recommended Portfolio[17]

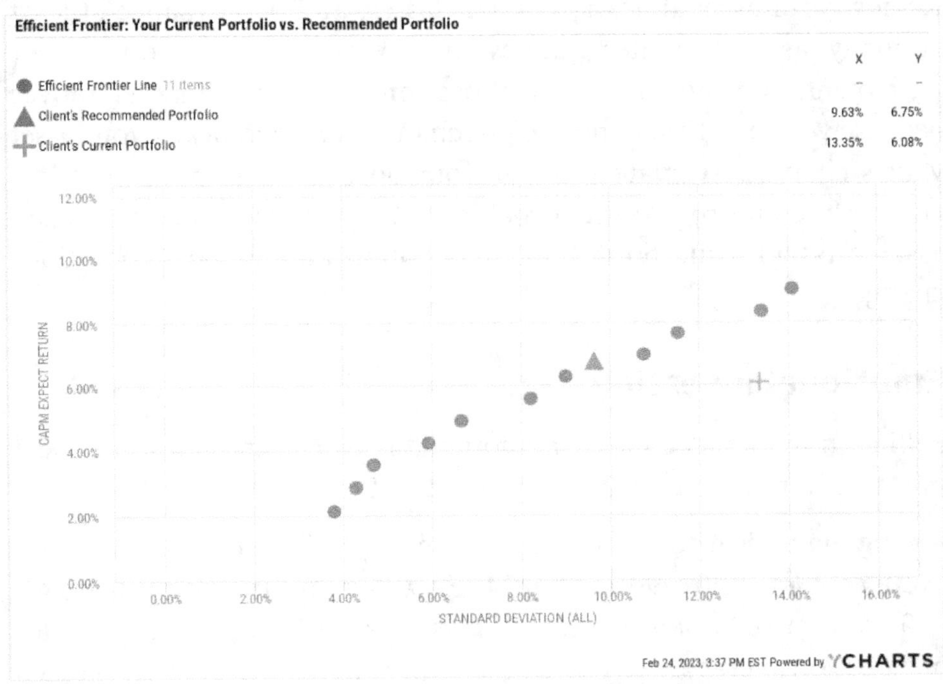

The example above is hypothetical and should only be used for illustrative purposes. This example is not based on an actual client experience or portfolio, but rather, it is intended to demonstrate hypothetical scenarios.

In this example the "Client's Current Portfolio" has an expected average return of 6.08% and an expected risk of 13.35%. The "Clients Recommended Portfolio" per the chart, offers a higher projected annual return of 6.75% and a lower projected risk of 9.63%. In this context, risk is defined as the standard deviation aka the *dispersion* from the mean return.

You may want to consider structuring a portfolio that can potentially generate the returns needed to meet reasonable goals while assuming an appropriate level of risk for your specific situation. Remember your portfolio should be customized to your specific needs.

Monitoring and Adjusting Your Investments

Review your asset allocation, asset classes, and performance at least annually, as well as after a life event such as a marriage, divorce, or retirement. Revisit your asset allocation after large market moves because your asset allocation might change considerably as your asset values change. Evaluate whether your portfolio continues to reflect your risk tolerance. Consider making changes to the weights of each asset class in your portfolio as economic and market conditions change.

Emotional Investing

Selling in market declines for emotional reasons can often times be a mistake. Market returns can be unpredictable.

As highlighted in the chart below, the S&P 500 returned 7.67% on average from 6/30/99 to 6/30/24. However, an investor in the S&P 500 who missed only the best 10 days in those 25 years had a return of 4.36% on average per year. Missing fifty of those best days produced a negative return of -2.30% on average per year. Think of the tradeoff between experiencing short-term market volatility and missing potential returns. Consider constructing a goals-based portfolio that will keep you invested during volatile times, rather than trying to avoid every market decline.

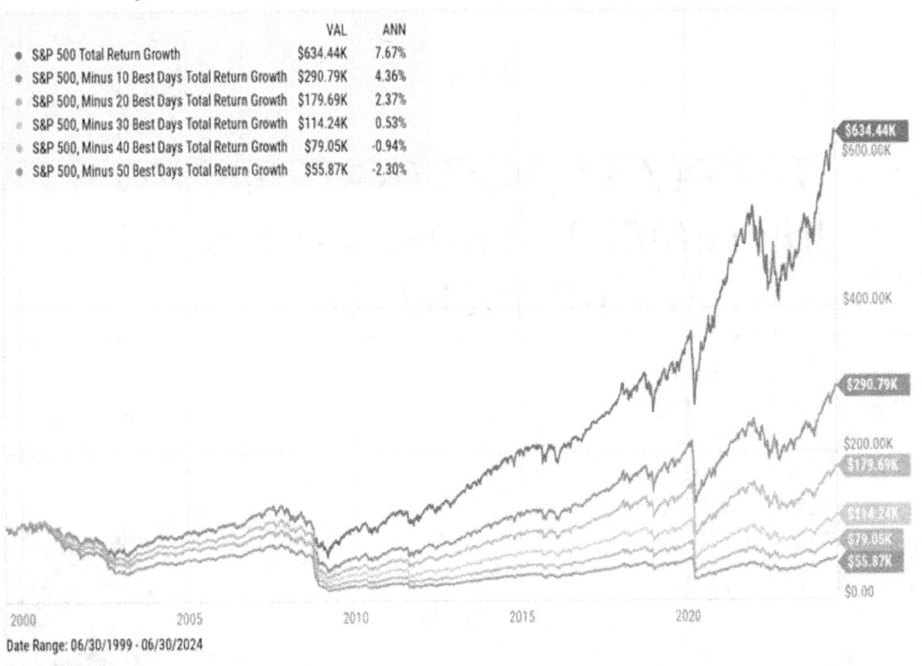

13 https://www.sec.gov/rules-regulations/2001/12/defining-term-qualified-purchaser-under-securities-act-1933

14 https://www.yieldstreet.com/blog/article/how-do-growth-notes-differ-from-income-notes/

15 https://www.yieldstreet.com/blog/article/are-structured-notes-for-you-pros-and-cons/

16 https://investor.vanguard.com/investor-resources-education/education/model-portfolio-allocation

17 YCharts. *Efficient Frontier: Your Current Portfolio vs. Recommended Profile.* [February 23rd, 2023]

18 YCharts. *The Effect of Missing the Best Market Days Over the Last 25 Years.* [July 2nd, 2024]

STEP 3

TAX PLANNING: STRATEGIES TO IMPLEMENT BEFORE AND AFTER RETIREMENT

Understanding Tax Planning in Retirement

You may want to have a tax plan that starts with leveraging the difference between tax deferred, taxable, and tax-exempt accounts.

You should be aware of the various strategies you can use to reduce your taxes. Finally, you should understand the power of tax advantaged accounts and how to manage the distributions from those accounts. Here, we will discuss each of these topics.

Marginal Tax Rates

Understanding tax implications in retirement starts with paying attention to your marginal tax rate. Your marginal tax rate is important because many of the strategies you can use are based on the difference between your current and future tax rates.

Marginal Tax Rates for 2025[19]

Rate	Married, Filing Jointly	Single
10%	$0 - $23,850	$0 - $11,925
12%	$23,851 - $96,950	$11,926 - $48,475
22%	$96,951 - $206,700	$48,476 - $103,350
24%	$206,701 - $394,600	$103,351 - $197,300
32%	$394,601 - $501,050	$197,301 - $250,525
35%	$501,051 - $751,600	$250,526 - $626,350
37%	Over $751,601	Over $626,351

It is important to note that federal tax laws under the Internal Revenue Code (IRC) of the United States are subject to change, therefore it is the responsibility of taxpayers to verify their taxation obligations.

How will your income be taxed? The following is a list of the most common forms of income and how they are taxed.[20]

Source	Tax
Social Security	Up to 85% of benefits taxed based on provisional income
Pensions	Ordinary income
Taxable Bond Interest	Ordinary Income

Municipal Bond	Exempt from federal tax. Might be exempt from state tax
Stocks, Bonds, ETF's (gains)	Long term: 0%, 15% 20%. Short term: Ordinary income
Dividends	Qualified: Long-term gain. Non-qualified: Ordinary income
IRAs and 401(k)s	Ordinary income. Withdrawals before 59½ may be subject to a tax penalty
Roth IRAs & Roth 401(k)s	Qualified withdrawals are tax-free

Tax-Deferred vs. Tax-Free vs. Taxable Accounts

You may own or consider owning a combination of individual retirement accounts, employer-sponsored retirement accounts, and/or personal investment accounts. You should be aware how each of these accounts are taxed and/or the tax benefits you receive from each of these accounts.

Tax-Deferred Accounts

Tax-deferred accounts, for example, are not taxed until you withdraw funds. Examples of tax-deferred accounts are Traditional IRAs, 401(k)s, and 403(b)s. These accounts typically provide a tax deduction on the contribution you make. The distributions, however, are taxable as ordinary income and subject to a penalty if you take a non-qualified distribution.

Tax-Free Accounts

Tax-free accounts include Roth IRAs and Roth 401(k)s. While contributions to these accounts do not provide an initial tax benefit, qualified withdrawals are not taxed and there are no required minimum distributions.

However, you should consider the long-term benefits of using a tax-deferred account versus a tax-free account, primarily based on your current and future tax brackets. If you expect to be in a higher tax bracket in retirement, consider making Roth IRA and Roth 401(k) accounts a priority. If you expect to be in a lower tax bracket in retirement, consider using traditional retirement accounts over Roth accounts. You can also allocate part of your retirement funds to each strategy. Work with an advisor and/or tax professional if you need help deciding which type of account is best for you.

529 to Roth IRA Rollover

If you have an overfunded 529 plan, consider rolling part or all of it to a Roth IRA. You can roll an overfunded 529 plan into your Roth IRA, your spouse's IRA, or to your child's Roth IRA. You can also name multiple beneficiaries. Be mindful of all the rules required to roll over a 529 plan to a Roth IRA.[21]

Health Savings Account

Another tax-free account to consider is the health savings account (HSA). Health savings accounts provide a triple tax benefit. Contributions are tax-deductible, earnings grow tax-free, and eligible distributions are tax-exempt.

Taxable Investment Accounts

A taxable investment account does not provide a taxable deduction when it is funded. However, there are certain investments you can purchase and strategies you can pursue to potentially reduce the taxes you pay in a taxable investment account. Next, we will discuss a few tax strategies for you to consider in your taxable accounts.

Tax Strategies for Taxable Investment Accounts

Tax Loss Harvesting

Tax loss harvesting is the process of selling losing positions in your taxable accounts to offset realized (and taxable) gains. If you wish to stay invested with the funds generated from the sale, consider purchasing another position in a similar industry. You can currently offset realized gains, or up to $3,000 in income. Track your capital losses, as any losses you cannot use in one year can be carried forward. Be aware of and careful not to violate the wash sale rule, or you will not be eligible to take a realized loss. A wash sale is when you sell a security at a loss and then buy it or a substantially identical security back within 30 days before or after the sale. [22]

Tax-Exempt Investments

Some investments, such as tax-free municipal bonds, are exempt from federal and state taxes (if you are a resident of the state where the bond is issued). Evaluate the after-tax yield of municipal bond investments based on your own tax rate and compare it to the yields of corporate or government bonds. This will help you determine whether a municipal bond provides the highest after-tax yield for you.

Long-Term vs. Short-Term Gains

Consider the difference between short- and long-term capital gains rates before you sell a security. If you sell a security that you held for a year or less, the gains on that sale are taxed at your tax rate. However, if you sell that same position one year after your initial purchase, your gains are taxed at the capital gains rate (0%, 15%, or 20%).

Asset Location

Be mindful of your asset location. Consider using taxable accounts for investments you plan to hold for more than one-year, municipal bonds, and tax-managed strategies. Use tax-advantaged accounts for investments you plan to hold for less than one year, actively managed funds that generate short-term gains, real estate investment trusts, and taxable bond funds.

Capital Gain Distributions

Be mindful of mutual funds that pay out capital gains right before the end of the year. Use an exchange-traded fund with a similar strategy if you wish to invest near year-end or reach out to the mutual fund company to inquire about any gains they may distribute before year-end.

Donor-Advised Fund

Another strategy you can use is a donor-advised fund.[23] A donor-advised fund may allow you to easily make a tax-deductible contribution to a qualified charity. You retain the ability to direct how the fund is invested and how the money is distributed to different charities.

Withdrawal Strategy

You should develop a withdrawal strategy around all your investment and retirement accounts. Consider taking annual penalty-free distributions up to your marginal tax rate to manage your future taxes or consider partial Roth conversions each year. A Roth conversion may be beneficial if a drop in income significantly lowers your tax bracket.

Tax Strategies for Retirement Accounts

Leveraging Tax-Advantaged Accounts

The best ways to leverage tax-advantaged accounts are to start your contributions as early as possible, contribute as much as possible, and maintain an allocation that aligns with your goals while providing a comfortable level of risk for you.

Qualified Charitable Distributions

If you are charitably inclined and planning to take distributions from your IRA, consider a qualified charitable distribution (QCD) directly from your IRA to a qualified charity. The distribution can satisfy part or all of your required minimum distribution and is not subject to taxation. You must be 70½ or older to make a QCD, and the distribution amount is limited to $105,000 (2024). You can even elect to use your QCD (one time only) to fund a charitable remainder unitrust, charitable remainder annuity trust, or charitable gift annuity.[24]

Qualified Longevity Annuity Contract

You can also purchase a qualified longevity annuity contract (QLAC) with some of your retirement funds.[25] The QLAC was enacted under the Secure 2.0 Act. You won't need to take distributions from that annuity contract until you turn 85. A QLAC could help you defer some of your required minimum distributions and tax bills from those distributions.

Net Unrealized Appreciation

If you own a large position of employer stock in a retirement account, consider the net unrealized appreciation rule. The net unrealized appreciation rule allows you to pay ordinary income taxes on the cost basis of your employer stock when it is distributed to a brokerage account, and then long-term capital gains on the net unrealized appreciation.[26] This strategy could potentially offer tax savings compared to paying ordinary income taxes on future distributions. It's advisable to run the numbers with your accountant or advisor to determine if using the net unrealized appreciation strategy is the best approach for you.

Backdoor and Mega Backdoor Roth IRA

Other strategies to consider include advanced planning techniques such as the backdoor Roth IRA[27] or mega backdoor Roth IRA.[28]

Backdoor Roth IRA

The backdoor Roth IRA strategy, popular with high earners, is a way to contribute to a Roth IRA if you can't normally contribute to one because of income limits. The strategy starts with a contribution to a nondeductible IRA and is completed with a Roth conversion. Make sure you are prepared to pay any potential taxes on the conversion and familiarize yourself with the pro-rata rule before you make a Roth conversion.[27]

Mega Backdoor Roth IRA

The mega backdoor Roth IRA is another strategy you can use to potentially save more in a Roth IRA or Roth 401(k). The mega backdoor Roth IRA starts with a contribution to an after-tax 401(k). After the contribution is made, you can then convert that contribution to a Roth IRA or Roth 401(k). Your retirement plan must have the parameters in place to allow for the mega backdoor strategy. Make sure to discuss the tax impact of the conversion with a tax professional.[28]

Required Minimum Distributions

While not a tax strategy, it's important to be mindful of the distributions required in your tax-deferred accounts.[29] The rules can be complex, but the key is to avoid penalties for failing to take a required distribution. There are no required minimum distributions in Roth IRAs or Roth 401(k) accounts.

Tax Strategies for Business Owners

There are many deductions and credits available for business owners. Some of the items to consider are the Qualified Business Income Deduction and the Qualified Small Business Exclusion.

Qualified Business Income Deduction

The Qualified Business Income Deduction allows eligible owners of sole proprietorships, partnerships, S Corporations, and trusts and estates to deduct up to 20% of their qualified business income.[30]

Qualified Small Business Exclusion

The Qualified Small Business Exclusion allows business owners to potentially exclude up to 100% of capital gains from the sale of their small business, subject to certain conditions and amounts.[31]

19 https://www.irs.gov/newsroom/irs-releases-tax-inflation-adjustments-for-tax-year-2025

20 https://www.kiplinger.com/taxes/how-retirement-income-is-taxed#:~:text=How%20some%20income%20in%20retirement,you%20made%20after%2Dtax%20contributions.

21 https://www.savvywealth.com/blog-posts/2024-planning-opportunities-from-secure-act-2-0-for-ford-motor-employees-and-retirees?utm_content=304478038&utm_medium=social&utm_source=linkedin&hss_channel=lcp-80447154

22 https://www.investopedia.com/terms/w/washsale.asp

23 https://www.fidelitycharitable.org/guidance/philanthropy/what-is-a-donor-advised-fund.html

24 https://www.fidelitycharitable.org/articles/secure-act-2-0-retirement-provisions.html

25 https://www.kiplinger.com/retirement/qlac-secure-act-gives-this-annuity-a-boost

26 https://www.kiplinger.com/taxes/tax-planning/604591/net-unrealized-appreciation-a-hidden-tax-strategy

27 https://www.nerdwallet.com/article/investing/backdoor-roth-ira

28 https://www.fidelity.com/learning-center/personal-finance/mega-backdoor-roth

29 https://www.irs.gov/retirement-plans/plan-participant-employee/retirement-topics-required-minimum-distributions-rmds

30 https://ttlc.intuit.com/turbotax-support/en-us/help-article/tax-cuts-jobs-act/qualified-business-income-qbi-deduction/L69VZ4PjA_US_en_US

31 https://www.sba.gov/blog/qualified-small-business-stock-what-it-how-use-it

STEP 4

ESTATE PLANNING: HOW TO MAKE SURE YOUR ASSETS ARE DISTRIBUTED ACCORDING TO YOUR WISHES

The Importance of Estate Planning

Estate planning should be part of your retirement plan. A proper estate plan will help to make sure your assets are distributed based upon your wishes after your death. If you have a large estate, estate planning might also help you minimize estate taxes. Finally, estate planning can help you avoid probate, which is the process of reviewing and distributing your assets.

Estate Planning Fundamentals

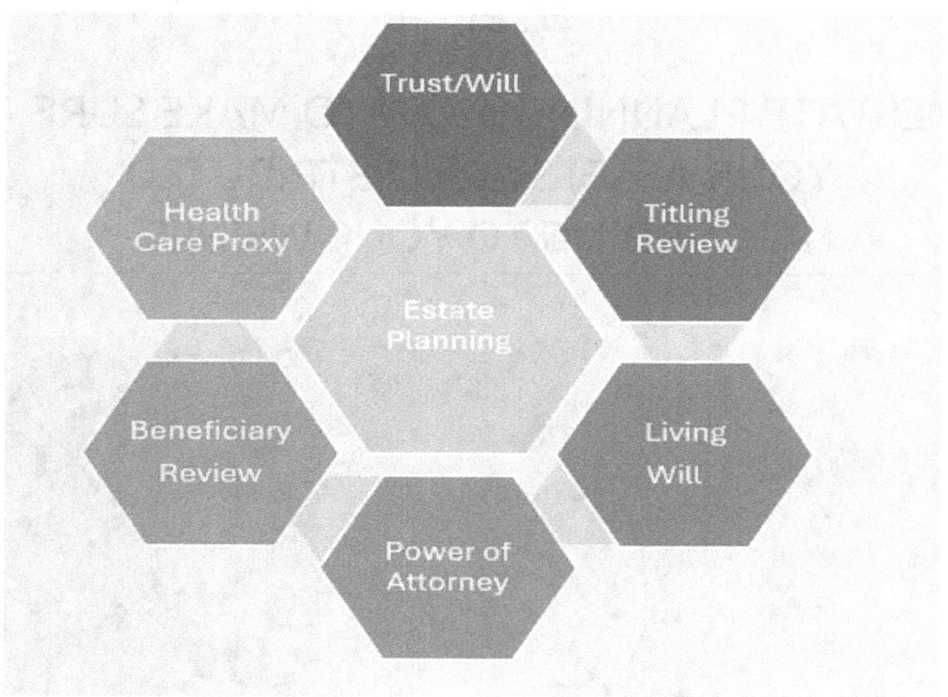

Wills

A will is a legal document that outlines how you want your assets distributed after your death. You should have at least a basic will in place. However, your will does not dictate the distribution of assets titled with rights of survivorship, retirement accounts, life insurance, or transfer-on-death accounts. Those assets are distributed to the beneficiaries listed directly on the account. Be mindful of which assets pass outright to beneficiaries, and make sure those beneficiaries are reviewed at least annually.

Revocable Trusts

A revocable trust can serve several different roles in estate planning. A revocable trust will allow you to manage your assets while alive, and then designate who will receive your assets after you die. A revocable trust also provides you with some privacy because the assets in the trust do not have to go through public probate proceedings. Make sure to move all your assets to the revocable trust and consider creating a pour-over will to capture any assets that may have been inadvertently left out of the trust.

Irrevocable Trusts

An irrevocable trust can play an important role in estate planning, especially if your estate is large. Unlike a revocable trust, an irrevocable trust is difficult to modify. If you create an irrevocable trust, you are giving up ownership of the assets moved to the trust. Those assets are then managed by a trustee. An important benefit of some irrevocable trusts is asset protection from creditors and lawsuits. Additionally, you can leverage the gift and estate tax exemption by moving personal assets to a trust. Consider consulting with an estate and/or tax attorney for more information about asset protection and how to use an irrevocable trust to maximize the gift and estate tax exemption.

Power of Attorney and Health Care Directives

You should also consider having a power of attorney, health care proxy, and a living will. A power of attorney allows you to designate someone to handle your financial decisions if you are not able to do so. The person you designate can perform tasks on your behalf, such as paying bills or selling property. A health care proxy is another important document to have. A health care proxy allows you to designate someone to make healthcare decisions on your behalf in the event you are not capable of doing so. Additionally, you can create a living will, which outlines your wishes regarding medical care. For example, you can specify whether you wish to withhold life saving treatments or dictate the use of pain medication.

Gift and Estate Tax

The estate tax is a concern for most individuals with large estates, with federal estate tax rates currently reaching as high as 40%. There is a lifetime gift and estate tax exemption, which is the maximum amount you can give away during your lifetime or at death without incurring an estate tax. While the current federal estate tax exemption is relatively high ($13.99 million per person for 2025), it is scheduled to revert to a much lower amount at the end of 2025. If you have a large estate, you may want to consider ways to reduce its size. There are several methods to reduce your estate size. Some of these methods include leveraging the lifetime gift and estate tax exemption, using the annual gift tax exclusion, and making direct payments to medical and educational providers on behalf of a loved one.[32] Next, we will discuss these methods and provide additional ideas for you.

Using Irrevocable Trusts to leverage the Lifetime Gift and Estate Tax Exemption

Irrevocable trusts can potentially reduce estate taxes.

Below is a list of trusts for your review.[33,34,35,36] Consult an estate attorney to determine whether one of these is suitable for you.

Grantor Retained Annuity Trust (GRAT): To potentially reduce taxes on distributions to family members.

Irrevocable Life Insurance Trust (ILIT): Used for estate liquidity and removal of insurance proceeds from your estate.

Qualified Personal Residence Trust (QPRT): Allows for the transfer of ownership of your residence to your beneficiaries while potentially reducing gift or estate taxes.

Spousal Lifetime Access Trust (SLAT): Potential for estate tax savings and indirect access to the trust.

Charitable Trusts: Enable donation of assets to charity while retaining an income stream.

Generation-Skipping Trust: May help reduce estate taxes and pass assets to grandchildren and later generations.

Crummey Trust: May provide estate tax savings and asset protection through annual gifts to a trust.

Intentionally Defective Grantor Trust (IDGT): Allows you to remove assets from your estate while remaining the owner for income tax purposes.

Gifting

Gifting is another effective strategy to reduce the value of your estate and potential estate taxes.

For example, you are allowed to give up to $18,000 a year (in 2024) to another person under the annual gift tax exclusion without reporting the gift to the IRS. If you are married, you are allowed to split your gift with your spouse, effectively doubling the amount you can give. However, if you choose to split your gift, you must file a gift tax return.

Exclusion for Medical and Educational Expenses

Another way to give to someone without having to declare a taxable gift is to pay their medical bills or tuition directly. However, be sure to follow all the rules required to qualify your payment for the exclusion.[37]

529 Contributions

A 529 contribution can help fund tuition for someone you love while reducing the value of your estate. You can contribute up to $18,000 a year (2024) to a single plan without impacting your lifetime gift tax exemption. You can maximize a 529 contribution to an individual's 529 plan by funding five years' worth of contributions in a single year. This will allow you to contribute $90,000 ($18,000 x 5) or $180,000 in 2024 if you split the gift with your spouse.[37]

Family Limited Partnership

If you are a business owner, consider consulting with an estate attorney to discuss a family limited partnership.[38] This strategy can enable you to take advantage of the annual gift exclusion by gifting shares of your business to others (such as children and grandchildren) in a tax-efficient manner.

Employee Stock Ownership Plan

An employee stock ownership plan (ESOP)[39] is another option for business owners to consider. An ESOP allows you to sell some or all of your business to employees in a tax-efficient manner. Consult with an advisor who understands the nuances of an ESOP before pursuing this strategy.

Planning for Wealth Transfer

Family Meetings

Annual family meetings are a great way to pass on your knowledge and values regarding wealth creation and protection. Consider using family meetings to teach younger family members about topics such as investments, taxes, financial planning, and which questions to ask advisors.

Estate Liquidity

You should be mindful of liquidity in your estate, especially if your estate has assets that are difficult to liquidate. We will now briefly discuss several liquidity strategies for you to consider. Consult with a tax advisor and/or estate attorney to discuss the additional requirements for any of these strategies.[40]

Irrevocable Life Insurance Trust

Consider purchasing life insurance within an irrevocable life insurance trust to provide liquidity for estate taxes while removing the value of the life insurance from your estate.

6166 Deferral

Consider filing for a 6166 deferral if your closely held business is valued at over 35% of your adjusted gross estate. The 6166 deferral allows you to pay taxes and interest pertaining to the business over a 14-year period instead of the standard nine-month period.

303 Redemption

The 303 redemption will allow for capital gains treatment on the redemption of your closely held business stock by the business.

2032A Special Use Valuation

The 2032A special use valuation for farmland allows for a reduced valuation of the farmland in your estate.

32 https://www.schwab.com/learn/story/estate-tax-and-lifetime-gifting

33 https://www.dominion.com/trusts/types-of-irrevocable-trusts

34 https://www.nolo.com/legal-encyclopedia/irrevocable-living-trusts.html

35 https://learn.valur.com/crummey-trusts-slats/

36 https://www.fidelity.com/viewpoints/wealth-management/insights/intentionally-defective-grantor-trusts

37 https://www.forvismazars.us/forsights/2024/02/simple-effective-gifting-strategies

38 https://www.investopedia.com/terms/f/familylimitedpartnership.asp

39 https://www.esop.org/articles/employee-stock-ownership-plan-esop-basics.php

40 https://www.comerica.com/insights/wealth-management/family-and-goals/building-a-liquidity-plan.html

STEP 5

LIFESTYLE MANAGEMENT: HOW TO LIVE YOUR BEST LIFE IN RETIREMENT

Defining Your Retirement Lifestyle

Money is not everything …. right? Regardless of whether you believe that or not, you should be conscious about how you want to live your life after retirement. What are some of the things you value most? Do you love to travel? What hobbies will you pursue or continue to pursue? Do you have an opportunity to give back by volunteering your time?

How about friends and family? Do your best to stay connected because loneliness can be a real concern as we age. According to a Meta-

Gallup poll (chart below), nearly one in four people worldwide feel very or fairly lonely.[41]

A Quarter of Adults Worldwide Feel Very or Fairly Lonely [41]

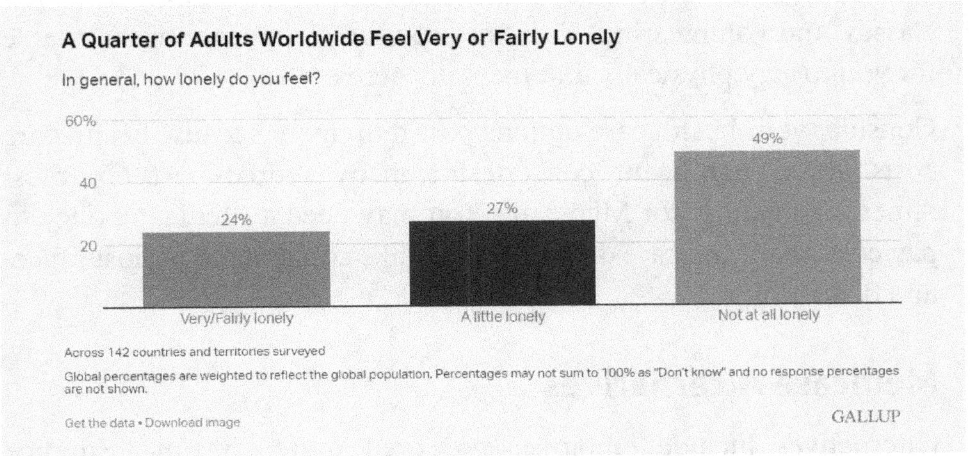

To combat loneliness, consider staying active in social groups, volunteering, staying in touch with friends and family, attending classes or joining a biking, walking, or running group.

Location

Where you choose to live will also play a big role in your retirement. You should consider issues such as the cost of living and proximity to family when deciding where to live or relocating. If you live in a large home, consider the advantages and disadvantages of downsizing to a smaller home. Other options to consider include aging in place or moving to a senior community.

If you choose to stay at home, make sure your home continues to be safe and ideal for you as you age.

Health and Wellness Considerations

You should be mindful of your health and wellness. Consider staying active, scheduling regular doctors' visits, and maintaining a healthy diet. Keep your mind healthy by reading regularly, attending free adult classes, and volunteering. There are countless opportunities available for you to stay physically and mentally active.

Consider your health care options post-retirement because health care costs are a significant concern for many retirees. At 65, most Americans qualify for Medicare. You may need a Medigap policy to pay costs that Medicare does not cover, like copayments, coinsurance, and deductibles.

Medicare Alternatives

Alternatives include employer-sponsored retiree health insurance plans, Medicaid, and health insurance through the marketplace established by the Affordable Care Act. Additionally, there are state health insurance assistance programs and services available for veterans through the Veterans Health Administration. Some of these programs offer free counseling and assistance to beneficiaries and their families.

Long-Term Care

Long-term care consists of a variety of services that can help you live safely if you have a chronic illness or disability, and may be provided by caregivers, family, friends, and/or care professionals. Long-term care insurance can help cover the costs of extended care, whether at home or in a facility. Start looking into policies in your fifties or early sixties when premiums are more affordable. Look for policies that cover a range of services, from in-home care to nursing home facilities. Medicaid can help those with limited assets, but it has strict eligibility requirements.

Hybrid Long-Term Care Insurance

Consider purchasing a life insurance policy that includes long-term care policy coverage. If you require care, the policy pays out some or all the death benefit while you are still alive. If you pass away without needing long-term care, your heirs receive the full death benefit of the policy.

41 https://news.gallup.com/opinion/gallup/512618/almost-quarter-world-feels-lonely.aspx

CONCLUSION

PUTTING IT ALL TOGETHER

Retirement planning can seem complicated, especially as we become increasingly responsible for our own financial future. By paying attention to these 5 steps— Financial Planning, Investment Planning, Tax Planning, Estate Planning, and Lifestyle Management—you can build a solid foundation for your retirement.

Recommended Next Steps

Financial Planning

- Create a goals-based written financial plan to determine the probability of meeting your objectives.
- Develop and review your balance sheet, outlining your assets and liabilities.
- Prepare a cash flow statement to analyze your current and future spending.
- Review all your debt. What interest rate are you paying? Can you refinance at a lower rate?
- Reduce your debt and interest payments by paying off high-interest rate debt first, paying off smaller loans first, or consolidating your debt at a lower interest rate.
- Review your Social Security statement and create a plan around your benefits.

- Review all your insurance policies to ensure you have appropriate coverage without being over- or under-insured.

Investment Planning

- Review your projected risk and return. Do you hold an optimal portfolio? Will your projected returns help you meet your financial goals? Are you comfortable with the level of risk in your portfolio?
- Consider if alternative investment options (such as private equity, hedge funds, or structured notes) could help optimize your portfolio and if they are appropriate for you.
- Create an emergency fund to cover unexpected expenses.
- Review your asset allocation. Are you overweight in any one sector or company?
- Does your portfolio align with your goals?
- Review the underlying costs of your investments. Are you utilizing cost-efficient vehicles? Are there suitable alternatives?
- Assess your strategies around stock options and restricted stock to make sure they are tax-optimized.
- Review stock concentrations. Consider reducing and/or liquidating your positions in a tax-efficient manner.
- Evaluate your cash positions. Are you earning enough interest on any excess cash?
- Review the asset allocation of your retirement accounts and taxable accounts. Are they aligned with your overall investment strategy?

Tax Planning

- Review your last tax return. What is your marginal tax rate? Do you have carry-forward losses? What was the ratio of short-term to long-term capital gains realized?
- Analyze your tax return to identify strategies that might minimize your tax bill.

- Look for tax loss harvesting opportunities in your portfolio.
- Evaluate asset location to determine if all your holdings are in the appropriate accounts.
- Make sure to take the required minimum distribution before year-end.
- Consider a Roth conversion to potentially reduce future tax liabilities.
- Explore tax-efficient vehicles such as donor-advised funds, charitable trusts, and qualified charitable distributions.
- Create a retirement distribution plan to optimize the taxes you pay on your annual distributions.
- Revisit the option of making a qualified charitable distribution from your IRA if you don't need all your required minimum distribution and are concerned about taxes.
- Consider a 529 rollover to a Roth IRA if you do not need the funds for educational purposes.

Estate Planning

- Create a will or revocable trust. Remember a revocable trust may allow you to avoid probate.
- Review the beneficiaries of all your accounts to ensure they are up to date.
- Take an inventory of all your assets and note how they are titled.
- Determine whether you may be subject to federal and/or state estate taxes in the future.
- Create and/or review your power of attorney (both financial and medical), living will, and HIPAA release forms.
- Develop a flow chart around your estate plan for clarity and organization.
- Consider working with an estate attorney to establish a trust if you require asset and/or creditor protection.
- Explore creating an advanced trust to potentially save on estate taxes if your estate may exceed the gift and estate tax exclusion.

Lifestyle Planning

- Take inventory of your hobbies and interests – can you continue to pursue them as you age?
- Consider where you plan to live. Is it optimal to stay in your current home when you retire?
- Look into joining groups to stay social.
- Stay active by taking walks, joining a gym, or signing up for a class that interests you.
- Create a plan to cover long-term care expenses.
- Develop a budget to account for health care expenses.

Final Thoughts

Your finances are made up of many moving parts, and each of these parts needs to be addressed in a comprehensive, customized way to ensure you stay on track toward your goals. Whether you are concerned about having enough income in retirement, creating a legacy for your family, or striking the right balance between your current cash flow needs and your long-term savings goals, consider a process that addresses all your worries, dreams, opportunities, and challenges.

ABOUT LOUIS GREEN

Louis Green is a wealth advisor with over 20 years of experience. He is passionate about helping his clients create comprehensive financial plans that allow them to pursue what matters most and feel confident about their future. Louis specializes in guiding business owners, executives, and retirees through their financial decisions, helping them avoid emotional mistakes and common pitfalls, especially during times of uncertainty and financial upheaval.

Louis aims to remain proactive in keeping his clients focused on their goals. He holds a bachelor's degree from St. Francis College and an MBA from the Zicklin School of Business at Baruch College. Louis is a CERTIFIED FINANCIAL PLANNER™ (CFP®) professional and also holds the Chartered Financial Analyst® (CFA®) and Certified Private Wealth Advisor® (CPWA®) designations.

When he is not working, Louis stays busy in his community. He loves sports and you can often find him watching the Knicks, Mets, and Nets.